Skills in English

Level 2

Reading

Terry Phillips

Garnet
EDUCATION

Published by
Garnet Publishing Ltd.
8 Southern Court
South Street
Reading RG1 4QS, UK

This edition first published 2003

ISBN 1 85964 782 0

British Library Cataloguing-in-Publication Data
A catalogue record for this book is available from the British Library.

Production

Project manager:	Richard Peacock
Editorial team:	Nicky Platt, Lucy Thompson, John Bates
Art director:	David Rose
Design:	Mark Slader
Illustration:	Beehive Illustration (Peter Smith), Janette Hill, Karen Rose
Photography:	AFP/Getty Images, Corbis (Bettmann/ Schenectady Museum; Hall of Electrical History Foundation/John Springer Collection), Digital Vision, Flat Earth, Image Source, Photodisc

Every effort has been made to trace the copyright holders and we apologize in advance for any unintentional omissions. We will be happy to insert the appropriate acknowledgements in any subsequent editions.

Printed and bound
in Lebanon by International Press

Skills in
English
Reading Level 2

Contents

Book Map

Theme	Reading text type	Reading skills
1 Education, Revise … But Take a Break	Magazine articles	• Revision
2 Daily Life, Parents, Adults and Children. OK?	Magazine articles	• Distinguishing fact from opinion • Applying ideas to real-world situations
3 Work and Business, How to Make Decisions	Magazine articles	• Dealing with headlines • Understanding non-text markers
4 Science and Nature, Chains, Webs and Pyramids	Encyclopedia entries	• Alphabetical entry • Reading for an established purpose • Making inferences
5 The Physical World, Comparing Two Countries	Travel guide articles	• Transferring information, e.g., text to outline • Recognising comparisons
6 Culture and Civilization, The Cost of Marriage	Newspaper articles	• Recognising the writer's point of view
7 They Made Our World, Genius and Perspiration	Magazine articles	• Reacting to a text
8 Art and Literature, *Julius Caesar* and *King Lear*	Narratives	• Following a narrative
9 Sports and Leisure, When Did They Start?	Magazine articles	• Identifying missing information
10 Nutrition and Health, Energy In, Energy Out	Articles Labels	• Revision

Introduction

THIS COURSE IS THE READING COMPONENT of Level 2 of the *Skills in English* series. The series takes students in four levels from Lower Intermediate to Advanced level in the four skills, Listening, Speaking, Reading and Writing.

The reading component at each level is designed to build skills that help students survive in an academic institution where reading research is wholly or partly in English.

This component can be studied on its own or with one or more of the other components, e.g., Listening and Writing.

The course is organised into themes, e.g., *Science and Nature, Art and Literature*. The same theme is used across the four skills. If, therefore, you are studying two or more components, the vocabulary and structures that you learn or practise in one component will be useful in another component.

Within each theme there are four lessons:

Lesson 1: *Vocabulary*
In the first lesson, you revise words from the theme that you have probably learnt already. You also learn some new words that you need to understand the texts in the rest of the theme.

Lesson 2: *Reading*
In this lesson, you practise skills that you have learnt in previous themes.

Lesson 3: *Learning new skills*
In this lesson, you learn one or more new skills to help you with reading.

Lesson 4: *Applying new skills*
In the final lesson, you use your new skills with another reading text. In most cases, the texts in Lessons 2 and 4 have a similar structure, so you can check that your skills have improved.

In this unit you are going to read two articles about learning.

Lesson 1: Vocabulary

You are going to learn some of the vocabulary you will need to understand the articles.

Ⓐ Complete each sentence with one of the red words. Make any necessary changes to the form of the word.

1 Are you _Consider_ getting a job this summer?

2 Did you do last week's English _assignment_?

3 Go to your student _advisor_ if you have a problem with your hostel.

4 I _respect_ my grandfather very much. He is a very good man who always helps people when they are in trouble.

5 My teachers at college are called _instructor_.

6 There are many different kinds of _intelligence_. For example, some people are good at Maths, some at languages.

7 Who do you usually go to when you want _advice_ about your studies?

8 You must work hard at college, but you must _relax_ too; take a break and enjoy yourself for a while.

9 You should always be _polite_, even if you are angry with someone.

Ⓑ Write a green word in each space to complete the dictionary entries.

1 _memory_ **1** the part of the brain where information is kept; *I have a good ~* **2** a particular piece of information; *I have no ~ of my childhood before the age of 5.*

2 _remember_ keep in the memory; not forget; *I can't ~ where I put my keys.*

3 _forget_ lose from the memory; not remember; *Don't ~ to call me later.*

4 _term_ **1** period of time – *In the short ~ you can remember a telephone number easily, but in the long ~ you will forget it.* **2** one part of a school or college year; *The next ~ starts in September.*

5 _brain_ the organ of the body that stores information and controls activity; *There is nothing wrong with his ~. He just doesn't work hard enough.*

6 _revise_ look again at information you have studied before; *Are you going to ~ for the test this weekend?*

Ⓒ Discuss these questions in pairs.

1 Do you have a good memory – for names, faces, numbers, facts?

2 Can you remember anything that happened to you before the age of 5?

3 How do you revise for an exam?

Red words column:

advice (n)

advisor (n)

assignment (n)

consider (v)

instructor (n)

intelligence (n)

polite (adj)

relax (v)

respect (v)

brain (n)

forget (v)

memory (n)

remember (v)

revise (v)

term (n)

Lesson 2: Reading

A Look at the heading of the text. Think of some answers in groups.

B Look at the graph. Answer the questions.
1 What is the title of the graph?
2 What does the vertical axis show?
3 What about the horizontal axis?
4 On the red line, how much learning is remembered one day later? 25%
5 On the orange line, how much is remembered one week later? 4%
6 On the green line, how much is remembered one month later?
7 What do you think the three lines on the graph represent?
8 Where is this information from?

C Look at the first paragraph. Complete this sentence about the text.
I think this text will be about ...

D Read the topic sentences of the other three paragraphs. What information do you expect to find in each paragraph?

E Read the text on page 4 of the Reading Resources book.
1 Check your answers to Exercises B, C and D.
2 Underline any new words and mark them *n, v, adj* or *adv.*
3 Do any underlined words mean ...
   a the noun from *lose*?
   b part of the verb *forget*?
   c look at again?
   d once a week, a month, etc.?

F Which is the best summary of the text?
1 You always forget things. It does not help to review information.
2 If you don't review new information regularly, you forget nearly all of it.
3 If you review information after one day, you will remember it for ever.

How Can You Remember Things for Ever?

Figure 1: % of learning remembered

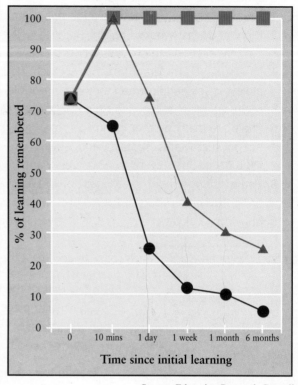

Source: Education Research Council

What happens after you have learnt something? Do you remember it for ever? Or do you forget it over time?

You forget it, of course (see Figure 1).

How can you stop this loss of information?

You must continue to review the information.

Lesson 3: Checking skills

A What should you look at before you start to read a text? Number these points in order.

_3_ Look at any illustration(s).

_5_ Look at the introduction / first paragraph.

_1_ Look at the title / heading.

_7_ Highlight the topic sentences of the other paragraphs.

_4_ Try to predict the content from the illustration(s).

_2_ Try to predict the content from the title / heading.

_8_ Try to predict the content of each paragraph.

_6_ Try to predict the information and order of information in the text.

B What should you do when you find new words in a text? Complete this diagram.

Figure 1: Dealing with new words

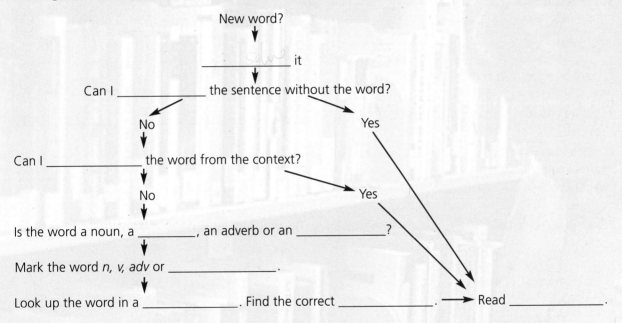

New word?

_____ it

Can I _____ the sentence without the word?

No   Yes

Can I _____ the word from the context?

No   Yes

Is the word a noun, a _____, an adverb or an _____?

Mark the word *n, v, adv* or _____.

Look up the word in a _____. Find the correct _____. ⟶ Read _____.

C What should you do after you have read a text? Complete each idea with words from the box.

| highlight   notes   picture   reaction   summary   vocabulary |

1 Write a _____ of the information in one or two sentences.

2 Draw a _____ or a graph of the information.

3 _____ important points in the text.

4 Make _notes_ of the information.

5 Add new words to your _____ lists.

6 Think about your personal _reaction_ to the information:

   a Do you think it is true, in general or for you in particular?

   b Will the information change your behaviour in any way?

D Read the text on page 4 of the Reading Resources book again. Then close your books and draw a quick graph of the information in the text.

E Will you do anything differently in your studies because of the information in this text? Discuss in groups.

Lesson 4: Applying skills

A Do the crossword.

Across

1 The noun from learn. (8)

2 To lose from your 7. (6)

4 To look at information again – another word for 5. (6)

6 The organ of the body that stores information. (5)

7 The part of the brain where information is kept. (6)

Down

1 The opposite of short-term. (4-4)

3 To keep in your 7. (8)

5 To look at information again, particularly for a test. (6)

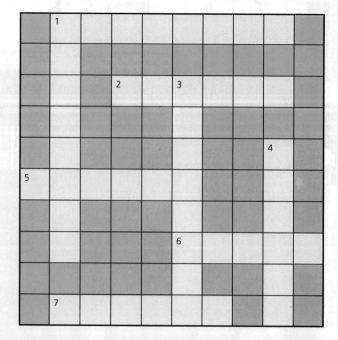

B You are going to read another text about memory. What are you going to do …

1 before you read? (There are at least eight things!)

2 while you read?

3 after you have read?

Discuss in pairs.

C Read the text on page 5 of the Reading Resources book. Do all the things you have talked about in Exercise B above.

D Work in groups. Compare your ….

1 summaries.

2 highlighted points / notes.

3 underlined words.

E Will the information in this text change your behaviour? Discuss in groups.

F Work in pairs.

Student A

1 Look at the graph on page 4 of the Reading Resources book. Describe it to your partner.

2 Draw the graph that Student B describes.

Student B

1 Draw the graph that Student A describes.

2 Look at the graph on page 5 of the Reading Resources book. Describe it to your partner.

In this unit you are going to read two articles about relationships.

Lesson 1: Vocabulary

You are going to learn some of the vocabulary you will need to understand the articles.

A Cover the red words. Complete each word with something suitable. Make any necessary changes to the words. Check your answers with the red words.

1 Do you belong to any social cl_ub_____?

2 What sort of mu_sic_____ do you like?

3 Do you live on the ca_____ or do you live at home?

4 Can you play ch_____ or any other board games?

5 Do you prefer to play sp_____ or to watch?

6 Is there a good re_____ near the college?

7 Have you seen any good fi_____ recently?

8 Are you pl_____ to do anything special this weekend?

B Ask and answer the questions in Exercise A in pairs.

C Read the text.

1 Complete the text with a green word in each space. Make any necessary changes to the words. You can use the same word more than once.

2 Complete the captions with words from the text.

Relationships with other people are never simple. _Parent_ often have problems with their children. Husbands often say, 'My _wife_ doesn't understand me.' _Adults_ have problems with each other at work.
We can often understand the _relation_ between two people by analysing the way they talk to each other. A lot of conversations have the form of stimulus–response. In other words, one person says something – the stimulus – and the other person answers – the _____. Sometimes, the _respon_ is expected, sometimes it is unexpected. An unexpected response sometimes shows that there is a problem with the _relationship_

Where are my black shoes?	They're just outside the front door.
stimulus ➝ expected _response_	

Where are my black shoes?	Why don't you ever put things away in the right place?
stimulus ➝ _unexpected_ response	

D Which relationship in your life is the most difficult?

campus *(n)*

chess *(n)*

club *(n)*

film *(n)*

music *(n)*

plan *(v)*

restaurant *(n)*

sports *(n)*

adult *(n)*

child/ren *(n)*

husband *(n)*

parent *(n)*

relationship *(n)*

response *(n)*

wife *(n)*

Lesson 2: Reading

You are going to read an article about relationships.

A Read the title of the article.
   1 What do the three nouns mean?
   2 What is strange about the title?
   3 What do you think the article is going to be about?

B Look at one illustration that goes with the article. Answer these questions.
   1 Who gives the stimulus in Figure 1?
   2 Who gives the response?
   3 What do you think the stimulus and response are in this case?
   4 *Husband / parent* is quite easy to understand. But how can you explain *wife / child*?
   5 What do you think the article is going to be about now?

C Look at the caption.
   1 What do you think *P* stands for?
   2 What about *C*?
   3 What is the *transaction*?

D Read the topic sentences from the article and answer the questions.
   1 In which paragraph do you expect to find …
      a more explanation of the illustration? $\mathcal{D}$
      b more information about Berne's model of behaviour between people?
      c more information about problems with transactions? $\mathcal{E}$
      d more information about Berne's idea? $\mathcal{B}$
      e more information about Berne's life? $\mathcal{A}$
   2 Skim the text on page 6 of the Reading Resources book and check your ideas.

E Read the text on page 6 of the Reading Resources book. Guess the meaning of the words in the box.

   | arise founded brain rebel |
   | switching workmates |

F Explain Figure 2 on page 6 of the Reading Resources book in pairs.

G Do you agree with the model? Give examples of conversations from your own life.

Are You a Parent, an Adult or a Child?

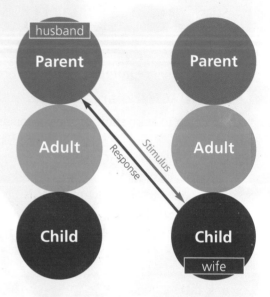

Figure 1: *An example P-C transaction*

$\mathcal{A}$ Eric Berne was born in 1910 in Montreal, Canada.

$\mathcal{B}$ Berne's new idea was that people have problems in their life because of their relationships with other people.

$\mathcal{C}$ Berne developed a simple model of the behaviour between people.

$\mathcal{D}$ We can see an example of a P-C transaction in Figure 1.

$\mathcal{E}$ However, problems often arise in transactions.

Lesson 3: Learning new skills

A Match the verbs and the words to make phrases from the article on page 6 of the Reading Resources book.

verbs	other words
1 train	**a** a new idea
2 practise	**b** a role
3 move	**c** a school
4 join	**d** as a psychiatrist
5 develop	**e** like an adult
6 found	**f** psychiatry
7 play	**g** the army
8 behave	**h** to New York

B Fact … or opinion?

1 Read Skills Check 1.

2 These statements are from the article. Mark each one *F* for fact or *O* for opinion.

   a ___ Berne founded a school of psychiatry.

   b ___ People always behave in one of three ways.

   c ___ Berne died in California in 1970.

   d ___ People often play games with their friends, family and workmates.

   e ___ There was a strong demand for psychiatrists during the Second World War.

3 Find more facts and opinions in the article on page 6 of the Reading Resources book.

C Applying ideas.

1 Study conversation A. What is the relationship between the husband and wife in this transaction? Use Berne's letters, P, C and A.

A

Husband:	You shouldn't spend so much money on clothes.
Wife:	Yes, I know. I'm sorry. I'll be more careful.

2 Read Skills Check 2.

3 Study conversations B, C and D. Mark them P-C, C-P or A-A.

4 Study conversation E. What is happening here?

Distinguishing fact from opinion

Articles often contain statements of **fact** and statements of **opinion**.

Examples:

Fact	*Berne was born in 1910.*
Opinion	*(Berne believed that) problems arise because of transactions between people.*

Sometimes there is an introductory verb with opinions – *believe, explain, point out,* etc. Sometimes you have to work out whether the statement is fact or opinion.

Applying ideas to real-world situations

When we read about ideas in psychiatry or any other field, we must always think:
Can I apply this idea to real-world situations?

Example:

Text	*In Figure 1, the husband is the Parent and the wife is the Child.*
Possible real-world example	*Husband: You should be more careful with money.* *Wife: I know. I'm sorry.*

B

Wife:	You can't go out in that shirt. I'll iron another one for you.
Husband:	Thanks. I don't know what I'd do without you.

C

Husband:	What shall we do this evening?
Wife:	Let's go to a restaurant.

D

Husband:	I don't know what to wear.
Wife:	I've put some clothes out for you.

E

Wife:	Where shall we go at the weekend?
Husband:	Why do I have to make all the decisions?

Lesson 4: Applying new skills

A Study the words in the box.
   1 What is unusual about them?
   2 Give two common meanings of each word.

a train	**c** found	**e** point
b play	**d** school	**f** model

B You are going to read another article about relationships. What are you going to do before you read the whole article?
   1 Number the actions in the purple box in order.
   2 Do the actions in the order you have decided. After each action, stop and think about this question in pairs: *What will the article be about?*
   The article is on page 7 of the Reading Resources book.

___ Find and underline the topic sentences.

___ Look at the illustration(s).

___ Read the captions of the illustration(s).

___ Read the title.

___ Read the topic sentences.

C Read the article. Answer these questions. You will need to put two pieces of information together in some cases.
   1 How old is Thomas Harris?
   2 What is the relationship between Harris and Berne?
   3 What is the name of the model discussed in this article?
   4 Which type of relationship do people have when they are young?
   5 What sometimes happens as people grow up?
   6 Why is Relationship Type 1 healthy?
   7 How do Berne and Harris feel about the other types of relationship?
   8 How can you move from Relationship Type 2 to Relationship Type 1?
   9 How can you move from Relationship Type 3 to Relationship Type 1?
   10 How can you move from Relationship Type 4 to Relationship Type 1?

D Find in the article …
   1 three facts.
   2 three opinions.

E Match the statements A–D to each type of relationship, 1 to 4.

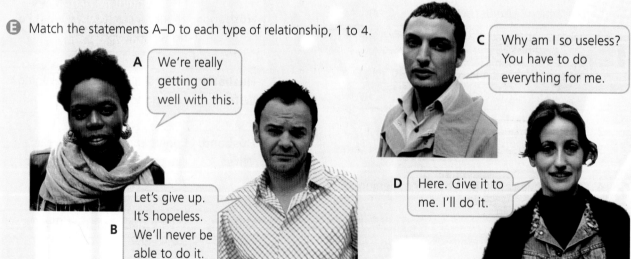

A We're really getting on well with this.

B Let's give up. It's hopeless. We'll never be able to do it.

C Why am I so useless? You have to do everything for me.

D Here. Give it to me. I'll do it.

F Do you recognise yourself or another person in the descriptions of relationship types? Explain your answer.

In this unit you are going to read two articles about making decisions.

Lesson 1: Vocabulary

You are going to learn some of the vocabulary you will need to understand the articles.

(A) Cover the red words. Write the name of the person that goes with each verb. Uncover the red words and check.

verb	person
apply	
assist	
employ	
lead	
train	

(B) Use some of the red words to make true sentences about you.

(C) Find a green word for each dictionary definition. Check with your own dictionary.

1 _____ choose an action after thinking about it; *The manager has to ~ who to employ.*

2 _____ work out the good and bad things about an idea, person, etc.; *I have to ~ the applicants.*

3 _____ a formal word for choose; *Which trainee did you ~ for the sales job?*

4 _____ 1. think something is true; *I ~ you are angry about losing your job.* 2. think of something as an example; *~ that you have got a new job.*

5 _____ the answer to a problem; *I can't find a good ~ to this problem.*

6 _____ a number of stages in a particular activity; *Choosing a new employee is a long ~, beginning with the advertisement and ending with the successful applicant being offered the job.*

7 _____ a number of letters that represent an organisation, e.g. WHO = World Health Organisation; you can normally say an ~ as a word.

8 _____ 1. make: *We use this machine to ~ electricity.* 2. think of: *You have to ~ several ideas before deciding which is the best one.*

(D) What is the process for getting into your college or university? What do you have to decide during the process?

applicant *(n)*

apply *(v)*

assist *(v)*

assistant *(n)*

employ *(v)*

employee *(n)*

lead *(v)*

leader *(n)*

train *(v)*

trainee *(n)*

acronym *(n)*

decide *(v)*

evaluate *(v)*

generate *(v)*

imagine *(v)*

process *(n)*

select *(v)*

solution *(n)*

Lesson 2: Reading

Ⓐ Discuss in groups.

1 What was the last big decision you had to make?

2 How did you make the decision?

3 Do you regret the decision now?

Ⓑ You are going to read an article. Look at the headline, subheading and table from the article.

1 What do think the article will be about?

2 What do you think it will say? Make at least one sentence beginning: *You should …*

Ⓒ The writer made a plan for the article.

1 Read the writing plan.

2 Read the topic sentences (under Table 1).

3 Number the topic sentences in the correct order, according to the writing plan.

Writing plan:

1. Introduction
2. Introduction of DIGEST
3. The process of good decision-making
4. An example of good decision-making
5. Conclusion

Decisions, Decisions, Decisions

'Digest' problems to make good decisions

Table 1: The DIGEST process

D	efine the problem
I	magine a successful solution
G	enerate alternative possibilities
E	valuate the possibilities
S	elect the best one
T	ell people your decision

Firstly, **define** the problem.

How do you make decisions?

Let's work through an example of the process in action.

We can summarise the process of good decision-making in the acronym DIGEST.

You will not make perfect decisions every time, even with this decision-making process.

Ⓓ Read the article on page 8 of the Reading Resources book. True or false?

1 ___ Using *gut feeling* and *instinct* means not really thinking about something.

2 ___ Good decision-making only really matters in business.

3 ___ DIGEST is the acronym for a decision-making process.

4 ___ The writer has chosen the acronym because *digest* means *to break down food in the stomach*.

5 ___ *Generate alternative solutions* means *think of different answers to the problem*.

6 ___ You should evaluate each solution as you think of it.

7 ___ The last stage of the process is selecting the best solution.

8 ___ The writer thinks it is better not to make a decision than to make a bad one.

Ⓔ Think about the example situation from this article (Paragraph 4). Go through the DIGEST process in pairs. Tell the other pairs your decision.

Lesson 3: Learning new skills

A What does the acronym DIGEST stand for? Test each other in pairs. Use Table 1 (page 8 of the Reading Resources book).

B Match each statement to one stage of the DIGEST process. _____
  1 I could _____
  2 I have to   _Define_
  3 I'm going to _____
  4 If I do that _____
  5 It would be good if _____
  6 The best idea is _____

C Look again at the subheading of the article.
  1 Why is it difficult to understand this subheading?
  2 Read Skills Check 1. Check your ideas.
  3 What should you do if a headline or subheading is difficult to understand?

D Look below at parts of the article.
  1 What do they all have in common?
  2 Look at the first part of Skills Check 2 and check your ideas.
  3 Identify each kind of non-text marker in the examples a – g below, e.g., _There is an acronym in sentence a._
  4 Find more examples of non-text markers in the article on page 8 of the Reading Resources book.

a What does DIGEST mean?

b … including 'to break down food in the stomach,'

c Firstly, **define** the problem.

d (If it isn't, go back to the first stage again and redefine the problem.)

e – look at each one carefully

f but you don't like public transport …

g The more people you _tell_ about your decision,

Skills Check 1

Dealing with headlines and subheadings

Headlines and **subheadings** can help us predict the content in an article. But some headlines and subheadings are written to make people think or to make them laugh. These headings are often very difficult to understand.

Example:
'Digest' problems to make good decisions
If you look up _digest_ in a dictionary, you will find the main meaning is _process food in the stomach._ This has nothing to do with the usage in the article.

Don't worry if a headline doesn't make sense to you. Read the article, then go back and try to understand the headline or subheading.

Skills Check 2

Understanding non-text markers

Writers use **non-text markers** to carry meaning. Here are some of the most common ones, with their meanings.

graphic	name	meaning
(word)	brackets	extra information
– word	dash	next information is a definition OR an example
'word'	speech marks	actual speech OR something that people say OR a definition OR unusual use of a word
word	italics	the information is important
word	bold	the information is important
WORD	acronym	the name of an organisation or idea
word …	suspension dots	the sentence is not complete

Lesson 4: Applying new skills

(A) Match the beginnings and endings of the DIGEST process.

1 Define	**a**	a successful solution
2 Imagine	**b**	alternative possibilities
3 Generate	**c**	people your decision
4 Evaluate	**d**	the best one
5 Select	**e**	the possibilities
6 Tell	**f**	the problem

(B) You are going to read another article about making decisions. Can you predict any of the content?

Study the items from the article. After looking at each item, discuss predictions with your partner.

(C) Read each paragraph of the article on page 9 of the Reading Resources book. After reading the paragraph, do the activity below.

Para 1 Define management style.
Para 2 Follow the instructions.
Para 3 Follow the instructions.
Para 4 Look at the table you made after reading Para 3. What is your management style?
Para 5 What is the best style to use in 'managing' family and friends?

(D) In business, what are the advantages of each management style?
1 autocratic
2 participatory
3 democratic

Are You an Autocrat or a Democrat?
It's all a matter of style

Table 1: An autocratic management style

Stages	Me	Them
D	✓	
I	✓	
G	✓	
E	✓	
S	✓	
T	✓	

Table 2: A participatory management style

Stages	Me	Them
D	✓	
I	✓	
G	✓	✓
E	✓	✓
S	✓	
T	✓	

Table 3: A democratic management style

Stages	Me	Them
D	✓	
I	✓	✓
G	✓	✓
E	✓	✓
S	✓	✓
T	✓	

What is your management style?

How can you identify your normal management style?

Imagine that you have to make a decision that involves other people.

The old style of management in business was autocratic.

So what are you – autocratic, participatory or democratic?

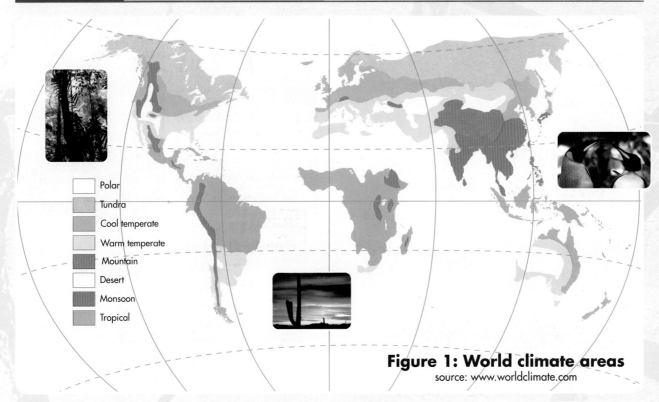

Figure 1: World climate areas
source: www.worldclimate.com

Map legend:
- Polar
- Tundra
- Cool temperate
- Warm temperate
- Mountain
- Desert
- Monsoon
- Tropical

In this unit you are going to read entries from an encyclopedia.

Lesson 1: Vocabulary

You are going to learn some of the vocabulary you will need to understand entries about science and nature in an encyclopedia.

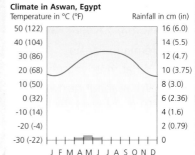

Climate in Aswan, Egypt
Temperature in °C (°F) — Rainfall in cm (in)

Temperature scale: 50 (122), 40 (104), 30 (86), 20 (68), 10 (50), 0 (32), -10 (14), -20 (-4), -30 (-22)

Rainfall scale: 16 (6.0), 14 (5.5), 12 (4.7), 10 (3.75), 8 (3.0), 6 (2.36), 4 (1.6), 2 (0.79), 0

J F M A M J J A S O N D

A Discuss these questions. They use the red words.
   1 What does a scientist do in a laboratory?
   2 What can you put in a table?
   3 What does the graph on this page show?

B Can you work out answers to these questions? They include the green words. Look at the map, the pictures and the graph.
   1 What does *climate* mean?
   2 What is the source of the map?
   3 What is the climate in your country?
   4 In which climate area do you expect to see penguins? And cacti?
   5 In which climate area are the rainforests of the world?
   6 *Living things* mean animals and what?
   7 What animals do you expect to see in polar areas?
   8 What about desert areas?
   9 What plants do you expect to see in tropical areas?

C Draw a climate graph of your area. Guess the information, or do some research.

D Make a list of animals and plants that you find in your area.

Red/green word list:
- graph *(n)*
- laboratory *(n)*
- science *(n)*
- scientific *(adj)*
- table *(n)*
- test *(v)*
- climate *(n)*
- desert *(n)*
- living thing
- plant *(n)*
- polar *(adj)*
- tropical *(adj)*

Lesson 2: Reading

A You are studying Environmental Management at Greenhill College.
Look at the list of lectures for this semester. Do you know anything about any of the topics?

Greenhill College

**Environmental Management
Semester 2**

Week	Lectures
1	Ecology defined
	Food chains
2	Food webs
	Food pyramids
3	The Greenhouse Effect
	Acid rain
4	Natural Cycles 1: Water

ecology The study of the relationship between living things and their ⇒**environment**. We learn from ecology that living things depend on each other to survive. This is because all living things are involved in ⇒**food chains**, ⇒**food webs** and ⇒**food pyramids**.

B Semester 2 begins next week. Read the information again.
1 What must you research this week?
2 What about next week?
3 When must you research *acid rain*?

environment The place where a group of animals and plants live. There are a number of different environments on Earth.

C You start your research with the entry for *ecology* in a science encyclopedia.
1 Read the entry. What other topics from this semester have entries in this encyclopedia?
2 Which of these other entries must you read this week?

D Read the entries for *environment* and *food chain*.
1 Make a list of other entries that you must read.
2 What else must you look at?

food chain This is the way that ⇒**energy** is transferred from one living thing to another. At the top of every food chain there is a ⇒**consumer**. This consumer is often a ⇒**carnivore**. This consumer eats another consumer. This is often a ⇒**herbivore**. At the bottom of every food chain there is a ⇒**producer**. If we remove one part of a food chain, there will be a reaction in another part of the chain.
(See Figure 1 for an example food chain.)

E Test each other in pairs.
1 What is *ecology*?
2 What is *environment*?
3 What is a *food chain*?
4 What is the relationship between *consumers* and *producers* in a food chain?

F Can you name some *consumers* and *producers* in your area?

Lesson 3: Learning new skills

A Cover the encyclopedia entries in Lesson 2. Complete these sentences with a word from the box in each space. Then read the entries again and check.

1 Ecology is the study of the relationship between _____ things and their environment.
2 Environment is the place where a group of animals and _____ live.
3 A food chain is the way that _____ is transferred from one living thing to another.
4 We learn from ecology that living things _____ on each other to survive.
5 At the top of every food chain there is a _____.
6 This consumer _____ another consumer.
7 At the bottom of every food chain there is a _____.
8 If we _____ one part of a food chain, there will be a _____ in another part of the chain.

| consumer | depend | energy | living | plants |
| producer | reaction | remove | eats | |

Figure 1: An example food chain

B Look at Figure 1.
1 Draw arrows to show the energy transfer.
2 Label the *consumers* and the *producers*.
3 If we remove the giraffe from this food chain, what will the reaction(s) be?

C You want to look up these entries from your research in Lesson 2.

| carnivore | herbivore | energy |
| consumer | producer | |

What order will the entries be in?
1 Read Skills Check 1.
2 Number the entries in alphabetical order.
3 Look up each entry on page 11 of the Reading Resources book.

D Work it out – true or false?
1 ___ A cow is a herbivore.
2 ___ A falcon is a carnivore.
3 ___ Man is a tertiary consumer.
4 ___ Energy passes from a producer to a primary consumer.

E Read Skills Check 2. What are your research questions for next week?

Skills Check 1

Alphabetical order

The entries in many reference books are in **alphabetical order**. You know the English alphabet already. But you must become an expert in the alphabet so that you can look things up quickly. Learn the rhyme from English schools:
A B C D   E F G
H I J K   L M N O P
Q R S T U V W X Y and Z
Remember: if two words have the same first letter, you look at the second letter, then the third, etc.

Skills Check 2

Doing research

Always read for a purpose. Write some research questions before you read:
Examples:
What is ecology?
What is a food chain?
Then go and do research to find the answers to those questions. Follow any links, e.g.,
⇒ **carnivore**, to extra information that will help to answer the research questions. Don't read anything you don't have to read.

Lesson 4: Applying new skills

A Draw a food chain with animals and plants from your area.

B Look back at the list of lectures in Environmental Management for this semester (Lesson 2). It is now Week 1.
1 What must you research this week?
2 Write your research questions.

C Find answers to your research questions. The entries begin on page 10 of the Reading Resources book. Follow any links to information that will help to answer the research questions.

D True or false?
1 ___ A food web is a connection between two or more food pyramids.
2 ___ There are sometimes 30 living things in a food web.
3 ___ A food pyramid shows energy transfer from the bottom to the top of a food chain.
4 ___ There are more living things at the top of a food pyramid than at the bottom.
5 ___ An ecosystem is an area with a particular group of animals.
6 ___ Only a change in climate can destroy an ecosystem.
7 ___ Climate is a combination of temperature and rainfall.
8 ___ Surinam, in South America, lies between latitudes 3° north and 6° north, so it has a tropical climate.
9 ___ South Orkney Island, near the South Pole, has a polar climate, which means the maximum temperature is 5°C.
10 ___ Photosynthesis happens in all plants.

E Look again at Figure 3 on page 10 of the Reading Resources book.
1 What eats what in this food web?
2 What are the producers in this food web?
3 What are the primary consumers?
4 What are the secondary consumers?
5 Find several food chains inside this food web.
6 What may happen to the living things in this food web if the giraffe eat all the trees?
7 What may happen to the living things in this food web if harmful chemicals got on to the grass, e.g. blown from farms by the wind?
8 Look at your food chains from Exercise A. Can you combine any into a food web?

F Look again at Figure 2 on page 10 of the Reading Resources book. Then read this text and draw a food pyramid from the information. Write the number of living things at each level.

At the top of this particular food pyramid, there is an eagle. This eagle must eat two snakes a day to survive. Those two snakes must eat ten frogs. The frogs must eat 27 grasshoppers. The grasshoppers get energy from eating huge amounts of grass.

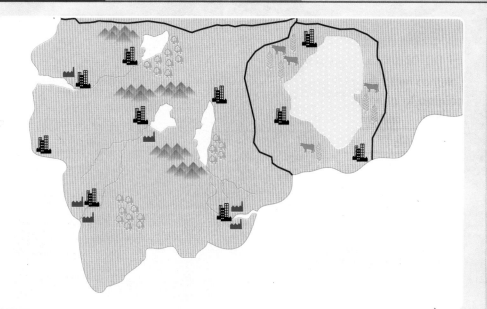

The following words appear in a vocabulary list alongside the text:

compass (n)

landscape (n)

latitude (n)

location (n)

longitude (n)

region (n)

the Equator (n)

the Middle East

area (n)

border (v)

climate (n)

industry (n)

natural feature

neighbour (n)

population (n)

In this unit you are going to read two articles that compare countries.

Lesson 1: Vocabulary

You are going to learn some of the vocabulary you will need to understand the articles.

A Answer these questions, which use some of the red words.

1 Which region is your country in?
2 Is it north or south of the Equator?
3 What is the exact location of the capital city?
4 What are the main types of landscape in your country?

B How can you compare two countries? Choose a green word or phrase for each space. Make any necessary changes to the words.

1 You can describe the location of each country and mention its _____ – the countries that _____ it.
2 You can look at the _____ – the number of people who live in each country.
3 You can consider the _____ – the size of each country, usually in square kilometres.
4 You can think about the _____ – the normal or average weather in summer and winter.
5 You can describe the _____ – the mountains, deserts, lakes and rivers in each country.
6 You can look at the main _____ in each country – what do they make or grow?

C In what ways is your country the same or different from **one** of its neighbours? Choose the neighbour and then use green words, *both* and comparatives – *bigger, smaller.*

Examples:

My country is smaller than Saudi Arabia.
It has a smaller area and a smaller population.

Lesson 2: Reading

Ⓐ What is your ideal holiday location? Make a list of things that the place must have, or that you must be able to do there.
Examples:
It must have a good beach.
You must be able to go skiing.

Ⓑ You are going to recommend to a friend somewhere to go on holiday. You have to choose between the two countries on the right. Look at the maps.
1 Can you identify each country?
2 Which region is each country located in?
3 What do you think is good about each country for a person on holiday?

Ⓒ You are going to read an article that compares the two countries. Look at the topic sentences. Check your answers to B1, and 2 above.

Ⓓ Read the information about your friend in the blue box.
1 Write a question for each point.
Example:
What language do they speak in each country?
2 In which paragraph of the article might you find the answer to each question?

Ⓔ Read the article on page 12 of the Reading Resources book.
1 Find answers to your questions in D1.
2 Choose one of the two countries for your friend's holiday.

Ⓕ Which word or phrase in the article means:
1 a place to go?
2 the natural things to see?
3 very high?
4 planes, trains, boats?
5 you can live there?
6 occupied?
7 send things to another country?
8 bring things from another country?
9 the average weather?
10 climbing mountains?
11 the broken walls of old buildings?
12 it's your choice?

Ⓖ Which country would you prefer to go to on holiday? Why?

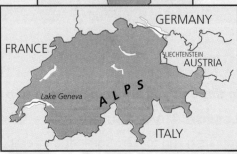

> What do you look for in a holiday destination?

> Tunisia is located in North Africa.

> Switzerland is located in Western Europe …

> Tunisia has a long Mediterranean coastline.

> Both Tunisia and Switzerland are small in terms of population.

> Both countries are agricultural.

> So why do people go to each country on holiday?

> It's up to you.

My friend:
- speaks French.
- likes water-skiing.
- likes mountain climbing.
- doesn't like very hot weather.
- loves fruit and chocolate.

Lesson 3: Learning new skills

Ⓐ Find an ending for each word from the article on page 12 of the Reading Resources book.

1	desti	**a**	able
2	lands	**b**	eering
3	trans	**c**	lation
4	habit	**d**	line
5	cli	**e**	stuffs
6	mountain	**f**	nation
7	coast	**g**	port
8	popu	**h**	rous
9	adventu	**i**	cape
10	food	**j**	mate

Ⓑ You are going to read the article again to find out factual information about **one** of the two countries.
  1 Read Skills Check 1.
  2 Think of some of the headings, e.g., *Country, Region, Borders* – for your table.

Ⓒ Work in pairs.
  1 Read Skills Check 2.
  2 Read the article on page 12 of the Reading Resources book.
  Student A
  Complete the information about Tunisia in the table below.
  Student B
  Complete the information about Switzerland in the table below.

Ⓓ Work in the same pairs as in Exercise C. Ask and answer questions to find out about the other country.

Skills Check 1

Transferring information into a table

How do you take notes from a book or an article?

You read	Switzerland is located in Western Europe and is bordered by Italy, France, Germany and Austria.
You write	*Switzerland is located in Western Europe and …*
or	*Sw = W E + It, Fr, Ge, Au.*

The problem with the first set of notes is that it takes hours!
The problem with the second set is that you probably won't understand them several weeks or even months later.
Make a table of information you want. Then read and transfer information into the table.
Example:

Country	Switzerland
Region	Western Europe

Skills Check 2

Recognising comparisons

Texts sometimes compare two things, e.g., Country A and Country B. Look for these signpost words.
both – this information is for A and B
whereas / while / however / on the other hand – the next fact only applies to one (country / thing)

Country	**Tunisia**	**Switzerland**
Region	*North Africa*	*Western Europe*
Borders	*Algeria (west); Libya (south-east)*	*Italy; France; Germany; Austria*
Area		
Population		
Capital		
Language(s)		
History		
Climate		
Agricultural land		
Highest point		
Lakes and rivers		
Industry		
Exports		

Lesson 4: Applying new skills

Ⓐ Factual texts contain a lot of information. But you can often work out even more information from the facts.

1 Read the Skills Check.

2 Read these facts from the text in Lesson 2. Complete each inference.

a Tunisia has a long Mediterranean coastline.

Tunisia would be a good place for a _____ holiday.

b Switzerland is land-locked.

Switzerland doesn't have _____.

c Tunisia is famous around the world for its dates.

Tunisia _____ its dates.

d Switzerland is bordered by … France
+ The country has three languages … French

They speak French near _____.

e Switzerland is famous for chocolate but … the cocoa beans are imported from South America.

They don't grow _____.

f Switzerland provides many opportunities for mountaineering – from gentle slopes to the highest peak.

You don't have to be an expert _____.

Ⓑ You are going to read about two more holiday destinations.

1 Prepare to read the article on page 13 of the Reading Resources book.

2 Read the text and choose the best holiday destination for you. Explain your choice.

Ⓒ Work in pairs. Read the article on page 13 of the Reading Resources book again.

Student A
Complete the information about Cyprus in the table below.

Student B
Complete the information about Sri Lanka in the table below.

> ### Skills Check
>
> #### Making inferences
>
> An inference is something that you think is true because of facts in a text.
> **Example:**
>
> | Fact: | Tunisia has a long Mediterranean coastline. |
> |---|---|
> | Inference: | *Tunisia would be a good place for a beach holiday.* |

Country	**Cyprus**	**Sri Lanka**
Region		
Borders		
Area		
Population		
Capital		
Language(s)		
History		
Climate		
Agricultural land		
Highest point		
Lakes and rivers		
Industry		
Exports		

Ⓓ Work in the same pairs as Exercise C. Ask and answer to find out about the other country.

In this unit you are going to read two magazine articles about traditional events.

Lesson 1: Vocabulary

You are going to learn some of the vocabulary you will need to understand the articles.

A Describe a traditional event in your country. Answer these questions.

1 What is the event called?
2 When does it take place?
3 What does it celebrate?
4 How do you prepare for it?
5 What happens during the event?

B Read the text. Then match each green word to its dictionary definition.

What is the difference between *wedding* and *marriage*? The two words are very similar in meaning, but there are important differences.

A **wedding** is an event. It is the time when a man, called the **groom**, and a woman, called the **bride**, come together to get **married**. It is the special **ceremony**, perhaps in a religious place, when the man and woman become **husband** and **wife**.

Friends and **relatives** – mothers, fathers, brothers, sisters, etc. – come to the wedding and, in many countries, go to a big **reception** afterwards with special food.

What about **marriage**? A marriage is not an event. It is the connection between the bride and the groom after the wedding ceremony.

#	Word	Definition
1	bride	a man who is getting married
2	ceremony	a man who is married
3	groom	a woman who is getting married
4	husband	a woman who is married
5	marriage	the adjective from *marry*
6	married	a meal and party after a wedding
7	reception	someone from your family
8	relative	a special event, often in a religious place
9	wedding	the joining of a man and a woman at a special ceremony
10	wife	the relationship between a husband and wife

celebrate (v)

event (n)

happen (v)

prepare (v)

special (adj)

take place (v)

traditional (adj)

bride (n)

ceremony (n)

groom (n)

husband (n)

marriage (n)

married (adj)

reception (n)

relative (n)

wedding (n)

wife (n)

C Discuss these questions in pairs.

1 When did you last go to a wedding?
2 Who was the bride? Who was the groom?
3 Where did the ceremony take place?
4 Was there a big reception afterwards?
5 Do you think it will be a happy marriage?

Lesson 2: Reading

Ⓐ Discuss these questions.

Are you married?

Yes

1 When did you get married?
2 Where did you get married?
3 Was it a big event? How many guests did you invite?
4 Did you get lots of presents?
5 Why did you get married?

No

1 When would you like to get married – soon, or after you finish your studies?
2 Why will you get married in the future?
OR
Why might you not get married in the future?

Ⓑ You are going to read a newspaper article about marriage. Look at the headline, picture and topic sentences on the right. What will the main point of the article be? Tick (✓) one.

☐ Many people are not getting married because it is too expensive.

☐ Governments have the answer to expensive weddings.

☐ A history of marriage.

☐ Marriage is expensive, but there are ways to make it cheaper.

☐ The cost of marriage around the world.

Ⓒ Read the topic sentences again.
1 What information do you expect to find in each paragraph? Think about this, then ...
2 Match each type of information in the blue box to the correct topic sentence.

Ⓓ Read the article on page 14 of the Reading Resources book. Check your answers to Exercises B and C above.

Ⓔ What conclusion do you expect to find in the final paragraph?
1 Discuss in pairs.
2 Read the final paragraph in the Reading Resources book. (It's upside down under the article.)

Ⓕ Summarise the article.
1 What is the main problem?
2 What are the solutions?
3 Does the writer mention any problems with the solutions?

Making Marriage More Affordable

Do you want to get married in the near future?

In many countries in the world, weddings are becoming extremely expensive affairs.

Young people in these countries know all about the cost of a wedding.

In some countries, men solve the problem by marrying foreign brides.

What can a government do about the problem?

Another possible solution is the mass-wedding – ceremonies with hundreds of brides and grooms at the same time.

Couples can save a lot by hiring their wedding clothes, particularly the bridal dress.

a	government attempts to deal with the problem
b	information about mass-weddings
c	information about the cost of weddings in different countries
d	information about ways the bride and groom can save money
e	introduction to the article
f	quotes from young people about the cost of weddings
g	reasons for (and problems with?) marrying a foreign bride

Lesson 3: Learning new skills

A What do the pronouns (in italics) mean in each of these sentences / phrases? Try to remember, then check with the text on page 14 of the Reading Resources book.

1 Even a relatively simple *one* can cost more than £50,000.
2 a sum paid by *her* father
3 But is *it* really a solution?
4 What can a government do about *it*?
5 *They* can be huge affairs, but all the couples share the cost.
6 However, *it* is only worn once and then put away.

B We have seen before (Theme 2) that we must distinguish fact from opinion.

1 What **facts** from the article do the numbers in the yellow box relate to?

50,000	44,000	3	hundreds
80	650	10,000	thousands

2 Scan the text on page 14 of the Reading Resources book and check.
3 What **opinions** about weddings do these people and organisations have? Some are in the article; for others you must make an inference.
   a Huda
   b Huda's sister
   c Nabilah
   d Some governments
   e Ali Salem
4 What opinions does the writer give in the article? Tick one or more opinions from the green box.
   a Find evidence in the article.
   b Read the Skills Check and check.

> ___ Weddings are too expensive.
> ___ Men should only marry nationals.
> ___ It is a good idea for governments to help couples to get married.
> ___ Brides should hire their dresses.

5 What is your opinion about the statements in the green box?

Skills Check

Recognising the writer's point of view

A writer usually has a point of view about a subject. A reader must recognise the writer's point of view. Why? Because it helps to evaluate the information the writer gives. If, for example, the writer thinks something is good, he or she may only give positive evidence. You need to look for information on the 'other side'.

From the article on page 14 of the Reading Resources book, we can infer a number of the writer's opinions.

The writer says	Possible opinion
even a relatively simple one can cost more than £50,000	Weddings are too expensive.
Is this really a solution? It may create a bigger problem …	Men should only marry nationals.
These schemes seem to be very successful.	It is a good idea for governments to help couples to get married.
It makes sense, therefore, to hire a dress for one or two days …	Brides should rent their dresses.

Lesson 4: Applying new skills

Ⓐ Match each adjective to a word / words to make phrases from the article in Lesson 2.

1	expensive	**a**	affair
2	huge	**b**	beads and crystals
3	wedding	**c**	bride
4	traditional	**d**	dress
5	foreign	**e**	expenses
6	local	**f**	reception
7	bridal	**g**	wedding
8	hand-sewn	**h**	women

Ⓑ You are going to read another newspaper article about marriage. Look at the headline, picture and topic sentences. What do you think the main point of the article will be?

Ⓒ In the pink box, you can read the next sentence from each paragraph. Match the topic sentence and the next sentence.

Example:

Nisha Sharma is an ordinary Indian girl.
She is a third-year student of software engineering at Indraprastha University in Delhi.

Ⓓ Read the article on page 15 of the Reading Resources book. Check your answers to Exercises B and C above.

Ⓔ Guess the meaning of these words and phrases from context.

1	extraordinary	**6**	stacked
2	arrested	**7**	brand new
3	union	**8**	attacked
4	matches	**9**	walked out on
5	illegal	**10**	refused

Ⓕ What conclusion do you expect to find in the final paragraph?

1 Discuss in pairs.

2 Read the final paragraph. (It's upside down under the article.)

Ⓖ Read the article again.

1 What is the writer's opinion of Nisha's actions?

2 What is the writer's opinion of the Dalal family's actions?

3 What evidence can you find for your answers?

Paying the Price of Asking Too Much

Nisha Sharma is an ordinary Indian girl.

However, on May 11th, 2003, this 21-year-old woman did something extraordinary.

The union between Nisha and Munish was an arranged marriage.

Nisha's family were prepared to pay money to Munish's family.

Nisha's father agreed to pay 15,000 rupees to Munish's father.

'Thank God the marriage did not take place,' said Nisha's mother.

Nisha's actions made the front page of newspapers across India.

Bride price is a big problem in India.

'What if they had hurt her or killed her?'
However, that was not the problem.
However, the actions of one brave woman may make a small difference.
In addition, there were 'gifts' from the Sharmas to the Dalals.
On that day, Nisha Sharma was getting married to Munish Dalal.
She is a third-year student of software engineering at Indraprastha University in Delhi.
This money is called a *dowry* by some people.
They led to congratulations from Indian government ministers.

In this unit you are going to read two texts about inventors.

Lesson 1: Vocabulary

You are going to learn some vocabulary you will need to understand the texts.

A How much do you know about space? Do the quiz and find out.

1 What is the name of the planet that we live on?
2 What is at the centre of our Solar System?
3 How many planets are there in our Solar System?
4 Which is the biggest planet?
5 Which is the smallest planet?

6 What is the name of the satellite that goes round our planet?
7 What kind of object is the sun?
8 What was the first animal in space?
9 Who was the first man in space?
10 Who was the first woman in space?

B Read the text, which contains the green words. Then find a green word for each dictionary definition below.

An **inventor** often works in a **laboratory**. He or she has an idea and builds a **device** to see if the idea will work. In many cases, the device doesn't work the first time. The inventor has to **experiment** with different ways of making the device, or with different **materials**.

Samuel Morse was an **inventor**. In 1840, he **invented** a way of sending messages thousands of miles by electricity. He called it the **telegraph** because, in Greek, *tele* means 'a long way' and *graph* means 'writing'. He registered his **invention** with the government and got a **patent** on it. This meant other people could not make money out of the invention.

The telegraph was the start of fast communication between different places. However, the invention of the telephone in 1876 led to the death of the telegraph.

	something made for a special purpose
	test something to check an idea
	create by thinking
	something created by thinking
	a person who creates by thinking
	a room for doing experiments
	things needed for a particular activity
	a document that says only the named person can make or sell an invention
	a device for sending and receiving electrical signals

planet *(n)*

satellite *(n)*

Solar System

space *(n)*

star *(n)*

the Earth *(n)*

the moon *(n)*

the sun *(n)*

device *(n)*

experiment *(v)*

invent *(v)*

invention *(n)*

inventor *(n)*

laboratory *(n)*

materials *(n)*

patent *(n)*

telegraph *(n)*

C Look at these important inventions in the field of communications. Guess the order in which they were invented.

Lesson 2: Reading

A Read this part of a short poem by an English poet. Explain it in your own words.

B You are doing some research into the work of famous inventors in the field of communications. Make a list of research questions. (Remember the serving-men.)

C You are going to read an article about an inventor. Some people call him the greatest inventor of all time.

  1 Look at the title. Check the meaning of *inspiration* in a dictionary. What do you think the other 99% is?

  2 Look at the pictures. Can you guess what any of the inventions are?

  3 Look at the first paragraph. Do you know what he invented?

  4 Look at the topic sentences. In which paragraph do you expect to find an answer to each of your research questions (Exercise B)? Explain your choice.

D Read the article on page 16 of the Reading Resources book.

  1 Make notes of the answers to your research questions in Exercise B.

  2 Check your answers to the questions in Exercise C.

E These statements are probably true. Find evidence in the text.

  1 Edison's mother taught him to read.

  2 *Hereditary* means something you get from your parents.

  3 The telegraph was used on the railway system.

  4 Edison knew people wanted the Stock Exchange device before he made it.

  5 Edison stopped working as a telegrapher in 1870.

  6 A tape recorder is a kind of phonograph.

  7 Before Edison, people made light bulbs with different materials.

  8 A digital movie camera is a kind of kinetograph.

I keep six honest serving-men
(They taught me all I know).
Their names are What and Where and When
And Why and Who and How.

Rudyard Kipling

One per cent inspiration

Thomas Alva Edison was born in Ohio, USA, on February 11, 1847. He moved with his family to Michigan when he was seven. Even then, there was an <u>indication</u> of his future life. 'He spent most of his time in the cellar,' his father told reporters later. 'He had a laboratory down there.'

Around 1855, Edison went to school for a short time.

At about the age of 12, Edison became almost completely deaf.

In 1862, the teenage Edison saved a little boy from being hit by a train.

He followed his own advice.

Edison's favourite invention appeared in 1877.

Edison went on to work on many more inventions.

On December 9, 1914, fire destroyed Edison's laboratories.

Edison died on October 18, 1931.

Lesson 3: Learning new skills

Ⓐ Do you understand these important words from the article in the previous lesson? If not, look them up.

> disability genius inspiration overalls patent perspiration

Genius is one per cent inspiration and ninety-nine per cent perspiration.

Most people miss opportunity because it wears overalls and looks like work.

I prefer the quiet of deafness to the noise of conversation.

I haven't failed. I have just discovered 10,000 ways that don't work.

Only invent things that people want to buy.

The present system (of education) … does not encourage original thought or reasoning.

Ⓑ Look at the quotes from Edison above.
1 Find each quote in the article on page 16 of the Reading Resources book.
2 Choose one quote and explain it in your own words.

Ⓒ You must always react to a text.
1 Read the Skills Check.
2 Which of Edison's opinions above do you agree with?
3 Look at the *Lessons for life* in the green box. Find an example of each one in Edison's life.

Lessons for life
If at first you don't succeed, try again.
One good turn deserves another.
God helps those who help themselves.
Concentrate on what you can do, not on what you can't do.

Ⓓ The article mentions three of Edison's most important inventions.
1 What are they?
2 What difference did these inventions make to the world?

Skills Check

Reacting to a text

A text gives you facts and, often, opinions – the opinions of the people in the text and the opinions of the writer. You must be able to distinguish fact from opinion (see Theme 2). But after reading a text, you must also react to it. Ask yourself some questions:
- *Do I agree with the opinions in the text?*
- *Which ones? Why (not)?*
- *What lessons for life (if any) does the text contain?*

Examples:

Opinion in the text	Schools teach children to memorize facts. (Edison)
My opinion	*I agree, but that is not true at college or university in my country.*
Fact in the text	Fire destroyed Edison's laboratory when he was 67, but he rebuilt the laboratory and went back to work.
Lesson for life	*You should not give up when you have a problem – at any age!*

Lesson 4: Applying new skills

A Match the two halves of these phrases from the article about Edison.

1	work	**a**	a fresh start
2	follow	**b**	a good lesson
3	miss	**c**	facts
4	make	**d**	long hours
5	memorize	**e**	an opportunity
6	invent	**f**	original thought
7	feel	**g**	advice
8	learn	**h**	strongly about something
9	encourage	**i**	things
10	spend	**j**	time (doing something)

B You are going to read another article about an inventor.

1 Prepare to read the article. Look at the title and the pictures. Can you guess the connection between the actress, the torpedo and the bar-code scanner?

2 Read the first paragraph and the topic sentences. Check your ideas from Exercise B1.

3 Do you think this article is about one person or two people? Explain your answer.

4 Do you know anything about the First World War or the Second World War?

C Read the article on page 17 of the Reading Resources book.

1 Check your answers to Exercise B above.

2 Why were these people important in Hedwig's life?
   • Fritz Mandl
   • Louis B. Meyer
   • George Antheil

D These statements about Hedwig are probably true. Find evidence in the article.

1 She was very intelligent.

2 She had many abilities.

3 She didn't like Hitler.

4 She lived to see her invention in use.

5 She realised how important her invention was.

E What lessons for life can you learn from the story of Hedwig's life?

The Actress, the Torpedo and the Bar-code Scanner

Hedwig Kiesler was born in Austria in November 1913. One year later, the First World War started. Perhaps her experience of growing up during a war had a strong influence on her later life.

In 1930, Hedwig became an actress.

Meanwhile, the world was heading towards the Second World War.

In London, Hedwig met a big Hollywood producer.

Submarines have special weapons called torpedoes.

The US Navy never used the invention.

Hedy Lamarr went on to make many more films.

Finally, scientists began to recognise Hedy Lamarr's role in radio technology.

Hedwig Kiesler died in Florida on 18th January, 2000.

In this unit you are going to read about two of Shakespeare's plays.

Lesson 1: Vocabulary

You are going to learn some vocabulary to help you understand the texts.

A Work in pairs. Ask questions to get the missing information for your text.

Student A
Read Text A.

Student B
Read Text B.

A

William Shakespeare was born on April 23rd _____. He was born in Stratford, a town in the centre of England. He is probably the most important person in English literature. However, we know very little about his childhood or early life. We do know that he did not go to university. He got married at ____ to Anne Hathaway. Their first child, _____, was born one year later, in May 1583. His twins were born in _____. He wrote his first play in 1589. It was called _____. In 1594, he moved to London. He became an _____, but he continued to work as a playwright. He wrote ____ plays altogether. People know his characters, including Hamlet, Romeo and Juliet, and Macbeth, all around the world. He wrote three kinds of plays – comedies, histories and tragedies. He died on his birthday in _____.

B

William Shakespeare was born on April 23rd, 1564. He was born in _____, a town in the centre of England. He is probably the most important person in English literature. However, we know very little about his childhood or early life. We do know that he did not go to university. He got married at 18 to _____. Their first child, Susanna, was born one year later, in _____. His twins were born in February 1585. He wrote his first play in _____. It was called *Henry VI*. In _____, he moved to London. He became an actor, but he continued to work as a _____. He wrote 35 plays altogether. People know his characters, including Hamlet, Romeo and Juliet, and Macbeth, all around the world. He wrote three kinds of plays – _____ _____ _____. He died on his birthday in 1616.

character (n)

comedy (n)

die (v)

history (n)

literature (n)

play (n)

playwright (n)

tragedy (n)

event (n)

origin (n)

plot (n)

source (n)

theme (n)

B Find and underline the red words in your text. Give a definition of each word.

C The green words are in the texts in this theme.
  1 Match each word to a pair of dictionary definitions.
  2 Tick (✓) the definition that will be used in this theme. Explain your choice.

_____ the main tune in a piece of music ☐ OR the topic of a play or novel, etc.☐

_____ the place where a river starts ☐ OR a person or document that provides information ☐

_____ an item in a sports programme ☐ OR a thing that happens ☐

_____ a small piece of land ☐ OR the main story in a play or novel ☐

_____ the starting point ☐ OR parents and grandparents, etc. ☐

Lesson 2: Reading

A Imagine you are studying the plays of William Shakespeare. This week, you are researching the play *Julius Caesar*. Make a list of research questions. (Remember the serving-men!)
Example: *When did he write the play?*

B Look at the illustrations and the title. Do they answer any of your research questions?

C Look at the section headings.
  1 In which section do you expect to find answers to your research questions?
  2 Do you think this text will fail to answer any of your research questions?

D Scan the text on page 18 of the Reading Resources book.
  1 Check your answers from Exercise C.
  2 Answer your research questions.

E These sentences are true. Read *Origins of the story* and *The real Caesar* and find evidence.
  1 Shakespeare wrote several plays about Roman history.
  2 *Julius Caesar* is a tragedy.
  3 Plutarch lived around the time of Julius Caesar.
  4 The English Channel separates Britain from north-west Europe.
  5 Julius Caesar died at the age of about 56.
  6 *Assassinated* means killed.

F Read *The play*. Number the pictures above in order.

G Read *The themes*.
  1 What are people persuaded to do in the play? Make a list.
  2 Why is each one 'against better judgement'?
  3 Which people abused their power in the play? Which people used power well?
  4 Was Brutus 'the noblest Roman'? What do you think?

The Noblest Roman of Them All

Origins of the story

The real Caesar

The play

The themes

Lesson 3: Learning new skills

A Match the characters in *Julius Caesar* and their actions.

1	Julius Caesar	**a**	have to leave the city.
2	Cassius	**b**	persuades Brutus to join a conspiracy to kill Caesar.
3	Calpurnia	**c**	reminds the crowd of all Caesar's good qualities and actions.
4	Brutus	**d**	returns to Rome in triumph.
5	Mark Antony	**e**	strikes the last blow.
6	Brutus and Cassius	**f**	tries to stop Caesar going to the Senate.

B How do writers tell the story of a play or novel?
  1 Read Skills Check 1.
  2 Tell the story of *Julius Caesar* in six sentences. Use the pictures to help you.

C How can you follow a narrative?
  1 Read Skills Check 2.
  2 Find and underline the examples in the text.

D What do these pronouns refer to in the text on page 18 of the Reading Resources book?
  1 him (line 19) _____
  2 She (line 41) _____
  3 him (line 48) _____
  4 them (line 54) _____
  5 he (line 65) _____
  6 He (line 65) _____
  7 him (line 81) _____

E Find and underline each noun / noun phrase in the article about *Julius Caesar*. Match the words that refer to the same thing.

1	Rome	**b**	mob
2	the Senate	**c**	the capital
4	assassinated	**d**	general
5	military leader	**e**	the government building
6	crowd	**f**	killed

F How does the writer replace the verb with a noun in these cases?
  1 The conspirators decide not to kill Mark Antony.
  2 She tries to stop Caesar going to the government building.
  3 ... the people who are backing Brutus

Skills Check 1

Following a narrative (1)

Writers often tell the stories of plays and novels in the present simple.

Examples:

*Julius Caesar, the general, **returns** to Rome in triumph, but important people in the capital **envy** his popularity.*

Skills Check 2

Following a narrative (2)

It is not good in English to repeat important words exactly. Therefore, writers often find a different way to say the same thing. There are several ways of doing this.

Use a pronoun*	**Gaius Julius Caesar** *was born in Rome around 100 BCE.* **He** *was …*
Use a different noun*	*Julius Caesar returns to* **Rome** *in triumph, but important people in* **the capital** *…*
Use a noun instead of a verb …	*Mark Antony persuades the conspirators to let him* **speak** *at Caesar's funeral. In his* **speech** *…*
… or a verb instead of a noun	*Julius Caesar is a play about* **persuasion.** *People* **persuade** *…*

*See Level 1, Theme 8

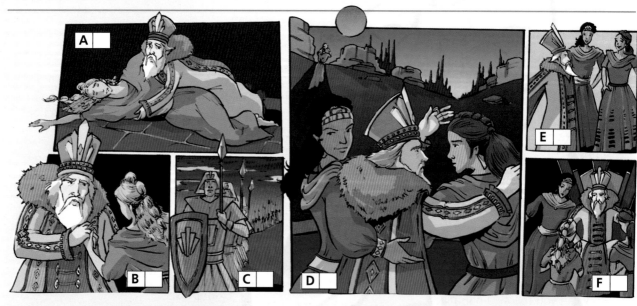

A
B
C
D
E
F

Lesson 4: Applying new skills

(A) You are going to read about another Shakespeare play. Complete these research questions.

1 _____ is it called?
2 _____ did he write it?
3 _____ does it take place?
4 _____ kind of play is it?
5 _____ is it about?

6 _____ does it end?
7 _____ did he get the story from?
8 _____ are the main characters?
9 _____ are the main themes?
10 _____ do people think of the play?

(B) Scan the text on page 19 of the Reading Resources book. Find answers to your research questions.

(C) These sentences are true or probably true. Read *Origins of the story* and *The real Lear* and find evidence.
1 Nobody knows exactly when Shakespeare wrote *King Lear*.
2 Nobody knows who wrote *The True Chronicle History of King Leir and His Three Daughters*.
3 *King Lear* could be called a history play.
4 Shakespeare knew the true chronicle very well.
5 Leir lived in or near modern-day Leicester.
6 Women could become rulers of ancient Britain.

(D) Read *The play*. Number the pictures above in order.

(E) Read *The play* again. Find each of the words below. Find another word later in the section that refers to the same person, thing or action.
1 king
2 change
3 becomes
4 divide
5 kingdom

6 happy
7 reject
8 sadness
9 invades
10 die

(F) Read *The themes*.
1 Make a list of lessons we can learn from *King Lear*.
2 Which one do you think is the most important?

(G) Work in pairs. Find and underline 10 pronouns in the text. Ask your partner what each one refers to.

In this unit you are going to read about two sports.

Lesson 1: Vocabulary

You are going to learn some vocabulary that you will need to understand the texts.

A Describe a board game from your country. Use some of the red words.

B Read the text.
1 Label the figures with some of the green words and phrases.
2 Complete Figure 4 with names of sports from the text.
3 Add one more sport to each group.

Do you play a ball game regularly? Millions of people in the world do. The most popular ball game is football, but volleyball, tennis, handball and basketball are also very popular.

All these sports need a net. In football and handball, there are nets at each end of the playing field, between two posts. In volleyball and tennis, there is a net across the middle of the court. In basketball, there are posts at each end of the court with a ring at the top. The net goes underneath the ring.

The rules of each game are different. In particular, there are rules about how you can move the ball to another player on your team. Can you kick it with your foot? Can you pass it with your hands?

Ball games with a net go into one of two groups. In some games, the objective is to get the ball *into* the net – the other team's net. In other games, the objective is to get the ball *over* the net.

C Discuss these questions.
1 Where can you play each of the sports in Figure 4 in your area?
2 Do you like playing or watching any of the sports?

Figure 1

1 _____
2 _____ 3 _____
4 _____

Figure 2

1 _____ 2 _____

Figure 3

1 _____ 2 _____
3 _____ 4 _____
5 _____

Figure 4: Ball games with a net

Ball games with a net

Objective: into the net / over the net
Examples: football / tennis

game (n)
land (v)
move (v)
objective (n)
piece (n)
play (v)
player (n)
turn (n)
ball game
court (n)
kick (v)
net (n)
pass (v)
playing field
post (n)
rule (n)
team (n)

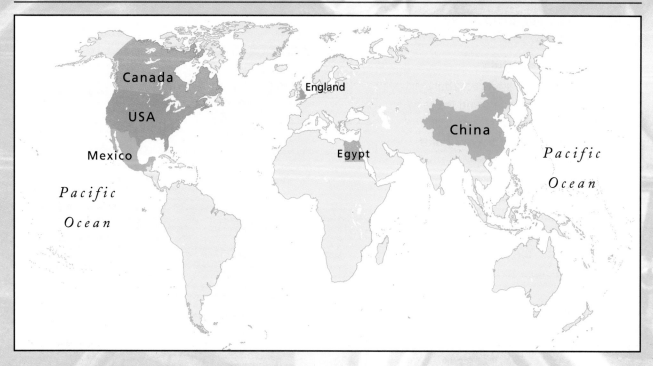

Lesson 2: Reading

Ⓐ You are going to read about the history of a game.
1 Read the headline. What is the game?
2 Read the subheading. What is the game?
3 Skim the first paragraph. Check your answer.
4 Explain the heading and subheading.

Ⓑ Discuss these questions. You will have to guess the answers.
1 Where did football originate?
2 When did the game start?
3 What equipment did the earliest players use?
4 Where did they play?

Ⓒ You are going to read about the origins of football.
1 Read the first paragraph.
2 What do you think will be in the next paragraph?
3 What about the third / fourth / fifth, etc., paragraph?

Ⓓ Look quickly at the text on page 20 of the Reading Resources book. Check your answers to Exercise C.

Ⓔ Read the text. Write on the map above the date of the first appearance in each of the named countries.

Ⓕ You want to make notes on the main information in the text.
1 What is the main information? People? Places? Dates? Make a list.
2 What is the best way to record the information?
3 Make a table. Read the text again and record the information.

Tsu Chi, Aqsaqtuk and Pasuckuakohowog

Are they the forerunners of the world's favourite sport?

The most popular game in the world is football. But where and when did people first play the game? There are many possible locations and many possible dates. One problem for historians is to decide the answer to a simple question: when is a ball game played with the feet actually a forerunner of football?

Ⓖ Which of the games in the text is the real forerunner of modern football? Explain your answer.

Lesson 3: Learning new skills

A All these words appear in the text from Lesson 2 (page 20 of the Reading Resources book).
  1 Match the words that refer to the same thing.
  2 Find in the text any words and phrases that you are not sure of. Check your ideas.

a location	**1** aim
b date	**2** bloodshed
c sport	**3** game
d started	**4** moved
e ancient times	**5** originated
f documents	**6** papers
g object	**7** move a ball with the foot
h passed	**8** regulations
i team	**9** side
j kick	**10** the old days
k rules	**11** when
l violence	**12** where

B The text could have sections with headings.
  1 Divide the text into sections.
  2 Give each section a suitable heading.

C The writer asks: *Are all these sports forerunners of football?* Skim the text. Which game might be the forerunner of each sport in the box?

ice hockey	rugby	basketball	wrestling

D What do the following questions have in common?
  1 What was the name of the ancient ball game in Egypt?
  2 When did *aqsaqtuk* start in Canada?
  3 What sort of playing field did the ancient Chinese play *tsu chi* on?

E Read the Skills Check. Check your answers to Exercise D.

F Read the text again. Make notes of the questions you still have to answer.

G Do some research on the Internet. Try to answer three of your sticky note questions.

Skills Check

Identifying missing information

When you do research, one book or one article never gives you all the answers. After reading a paragraph, make a note of the questions that you still need to answer. Use sticky notes in the margin of the text.

Examples:

Paragraph	Questions
Some historians believe that there were ancient ball games in Egypt in about 1800 BCE. They were part of religious ceremonies. However, there is no clear evidence that anyone actually kicked the ball.	name? equipment? playing field?
In the South Pacific in the old days, there were many ball games. In some games they kicked coconuts or oranges, while in other games they used their hands to pass the ball from one player to another. We do not know when any of these games originated.	ball? date? name? playing field?

Lesson 4: Applying new skills

A All the words below are in the text about football.

1 Match the words in each group to make phrases, e.g., *football ground/field*.

2 Check with the text on page 20 of the Reading Resources book.

Phrases connected with sport

a football	**1** ball
b playing	**2** field
c rubber	**3** game
d wooden	**4** ground
e ball	**5** post
f goal	**6** ring

Other phrases

a religious	**1** soldiers
b ancient	**2** ceremonies
c neighbouring	**3** continent
d enemy	**4** people
e white	**5** skins
f native	**6** Americans
g animal	**7** times
h American	**8** villages

B You are going to read another article about a sport.

1 Prepare to read the article.

2 Make a question that you expect each paragraph to answer.

C Skim the article on page 21 of the Reading Resources book. Find the answers to your questions in Exercise B.

D Make a time line of the history of horse racing.

E There is important information missing from each paragraph. Add sticky notes with a question about the missing information.

Example:

Nobody knows exactly when people started to tame wild horses. It probably happened some time around 3700 BCE.

Where?

F Here is some missing information. Can you match any information to one of your sticky note questions?

• called *Seglavi, Koheil, Manaki, Gilfi* and *Abu-Arkub*
• called the *Kikkuli Text*
• in 648 BCE
• in AD 470
• in an area that is now called Kazakhstan
• in the 8th century
• Omar Ibn Al Khattab

From Food to Farming, from Fighting to Flat Racing

The long, slow road to a short, fast race

One of the most popular sports in the world is horse racing. Horses race each other naturally in the wild, but men and horses lived side by side for thousands of years before anyone managed to get up on the back of a horse and ride it. Where and when did horse racing actually begin?

Before you can ride a horse, you have to catch it and tame it.

So men lived with horses for many years before someone had a good idea.

At the 23rd Olympic Games of ancient times, a new competition appeared.

Some Romans grew to love the new sport.

What about the Arab World?

We know that by 1600, people were bringing Arabian horses to England to improve the native English horses.

Nowadays, millions of people watch horse racing every day, at the track or on television.

In this unit you are going to read an article about energy and do some research.

Lesson 1: Vocabulary

You are going to learn some vocabulary that you will need to understand the article and the research information.

Ⓐ Look at the red words.

1 Which of these foods do you:
 a eat all the time?
 b eat occasionally?
 c never eat?

2 Which of these foods are:
 a healthy?
 b unhealthy?
 c not healthy or unhealthy?

Ⓑ Read the text. Choose one of the red or green words in each case.

In many parts of the modern world, we eat a lot of fast food. The most popular fast food is burger and crisps / chips. We also eat a lot of things between meals, like pasta / biscuits and bars of chocolate / cake. Children nowadays also eat a lot of sweets / cereal. These foods are not very good for us if we eat too much.

There are three main problems with fast food, snacks and sweets. Firstly, many fast foods contain a large amount of fat / carbohydrate. We need some fat, especially vegetable fat, but there is a lot of animal fat in a burger, for example. Chips are potatoes fried in fat / vitamins, so they are a problem, too. Secondly, many fast foods contain a lot of sodium chloride (NaCl), or salt. We need some salt in our food, but too much can cause problems. Finally, biscuits, cake, sweets and chocolate / pasta contain a lot of sugar. Once again, sugar is not bad in small quantities, but too much sugar can make you fat / fats.

The human body needs energy / protein every day. It makes the muscles / fat work, and that helps us to live and move. We get the energy from protein and carbohydrate / minerals in food. Protein comes, for example, from fish and meat, while fibre / carbohydrate comes from foods like bread, rice and pasta / burgers. We also need some fibre / energy in our food. We get it from fruit and vegetables and from cereals / chocolate. We need it, but we can't use it for energy. It passes through the body but, on the way, it helps the body to work properly. Finally, we need a small amount of vitamins and minerals / protein to keep us healthy. The main vitamin is C, from fruit like oranges.

| biscuit (n) |
| burger (n) |
| cake (n) |
| cereal (n) |
| chip (n) |
| chocolate (n) |
| crisp (n) |
| pasta (n) |
| potato(es) (n) |
| sweet (n) |
| carbohydrate (n) |
| energy (n) |
| fat (adj) |
| fat/s (n) |
| fibre (n) |
| mineral (n) |
| muscles (n) |
| protein (n) |
| vitamin (n) |

Ⓒ Look at the nutrition information from a product.
 1 What do you get from this product?
 2 Which of these things are useful?
 3 Which of these things are unhealthy if you have too much?
 4 What do you think the product is?

NUTRITION INFORMATION	
Typical composition	100ml glass provides
Energy	198.0kJ / 47.0kcal
Protein	0.5g
Carbohydrates	10.5g
of which sugars	10.5g
Fat	trace
of which saturates	0.0g
Fibre	trace
Sodium	trace
VITAMINS / MINERALS	
Vitamin C	25.0mg (42% RDA)
RDA = Recommended Daily Allowance	

Lesson 2: Reading review (1)

Ⓐ You are going to read a text about body energy. Make a list of 10 things you need body energy for.
Example: *You need body energy for breathing.*

Ⓑ In this course you have learnt to use illustrations, tables and diagrams to help you understand a text. Look at the illustration. Guess the main idea of the text.

Ⓒ In this course you have learnt to use the first paragraph and the topic sentences to get the main idea of a text. Read the first paragraph and the topic sentences. What is the main idea of this text?

Ⓓ In this course you have learnt to get the main point of each paragraph from its topic sentence. Write a question from each topic sentence that you expect the paragraph to answer.
Examples:

Topic sentence	Question
Let's look first at body energy.	*What is body energy?*
Most of the time we want body energy to be in balance.	*How can we make body energy balance?*

Ⓔ Read the texts on page 22 of the Reading Resources book. Find answers to each of your questions in Exercise D.

Ⓕ In this course you have learnt to write research questions, perhaps on sticky notes. Read the text again. Write some research questions.

Ⓖ In this course you have learnt to distinguish fact from opinion.
1 Find three facts in the text.
2 Find three opinions.

Is Your Body Energy in Balance?

If it is, your weight will not change. If your body energy is not in balance, your weight will rise or go down. But what is body energy? How can we make it balance? And what will happen if it isn't balanced?

Let's look first at body energy.

Most of the time, we want body energy to be in balance.

In some situations, body energy is not in balance.

Most people are happy with balanced energy, but some people want to have a negative balance.

The bad way is to go on a diet.

At this point, your body will go into starvation mode.

This is not a big problem while you are dieting, but you cannot diet for ever.

What about the good way?

This is a good way, but it is not the best way to lose weight.

Lesson 3: Reading review (2)

Ⓐ How are these verbs used in the text in Lesson 2?

1 Think of a word or phrase to go with each verb.

2 Check with the text on page 22 of the Reading Resources book.

a balance	*energy in and energy out*	**g** reduce	_____
b go back to	_____	**h** slow down	_____
c go on	_____	**i** store	_____
d increase	_____	**j** take	_____
e lose	_____	**k** use	_____
f put on	_____	**l** look up	_____

Ⓑ In this course you have learnt to transfer information from one form to another.

Read the text again on page 22 of the Reading Resources book.

1 Complete the diagrams that summarise the information in the text.

2 Close your books. Try to draw the final diagram from the information in the text.

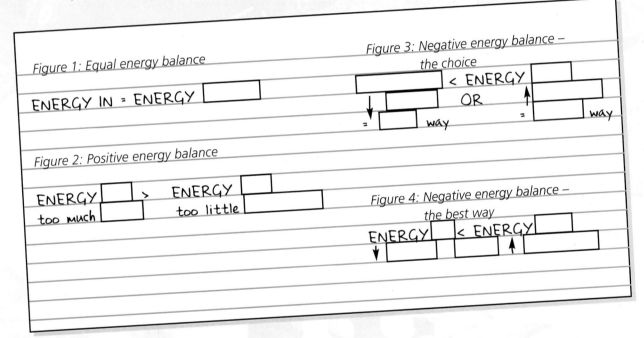

Figure 1: Equal energy balance

ENERGY IN = ENERGY ☐

Figure 2: Positive energy balance

ENERGY ☐ > ENERGY ☐
too much ☐   too little ☐

Figure 3: Negative energy balance – the choice

☐ < ENERGY ☐
= ☐ way   OR   = ☐ way

Figure 4: Negative energy balance – the best way

ENERGY ☐ < ENERGY ☐

Ⓒ In this course you have learnt to make inferences – to read between the lines.

Find evidence in the text for each of these statements.

1 *Rise* means *go up*.

2 The abbreviation for *kilocalories* is *kcal*.

3 *Lose* can be the opposite of *put on*.

4 *Positive* is the opposite of *negative*.

5 Your body normally contains more water than it needs.

6 People on a diet often become less active.

7 No diet gives you everything that your body needs.

8 Sportsmen and women need more than 2,700 kcal per day.

9 Your body needs carbohydrate and protein.

10 There are different opinions about the best way to diet.

Ⓓ In this course you have learnt to react to a text. You have also learnt to apply information to real-world situations.

1 Which information in this text surprises you?

2 Will the information change your behaviour in any way? If so, how? If not, why not?

Lesson 4: Reading review (3)

Ⓐ There are a lot of conditional sentences in the texts in Lessons 2 and 3.
  1 Cover the clauses on the right below. Think of a suitable way to complete each sentence.
  2 Uncover the endings. Find an ending for each *if* clause.
  3 Check with the text on page 22 of the Reading Resources book.

  a If your body energy is not in balance,
  b If the daily energy in is the same as the energy out,
  c If the energy in is greater than the energy out,
  d If the energy out is greater than the energy in,
  e If you go on a diet,
  f If you increase your physical activity,

  1 you will have a negative energy balance.
  2 you will have a positive energy balance.
  3 at first you will lose weight quite quickly.
  4 you will use more calories.
  5 your body energy will balance.
  6 your weight will rise or go down.

Ⓑ In this course you have learnt to read for a purpose.
  1 Look back at your research questions from Lesson 2 Exercise F. Scan the information on pages 22 and 23 of the Reading Resources book. Match the questions to the information. Move your sticky notes if you have used them.
  2 Find an answer to each research question.
  3 If you have new research questions, write them next to the information (on sticky notes if you use them).

Ⓒ In this course you have learnt to read information in tables. Answer these questions about the labels with nutrition information.
  1 Why do all the labels have '(per) 100g (provide)'?
  2 Which of the foods has the most energy?
  3 Which has the most sugar?
  4 Which has the most unsaturated fat?
  5 What sort of food does label A below come from?
  6 What about B?
  7 What differences can you find between Food A and the similar food?
  8 What about Food B and the similar food?

A

NUTRITION INFORMATION		
Typical values	Per 100g	Serving of 40g with 125ml skimmed milk
ENERGY	1499.0kJ 354.0kcal	853.0kJ 202.0kcal
PROTEIN	8.3g	7.6g
CARBOHYDRATES	68.7g	33.6g
of which sugars	25.1g	15.9g
FAT	5.1g	4.1g
of which saturates	2.5g	2.2g
FIBRE	8.9g	3.6g
SODIUM	Trace	Trace

B

NUTRITION INFORMATION		
Typical analysis	Per slice (40g)	Per 100g
Energy	377.0kJ 89.0kcal	943.0kJ 222.0kcal
Protein	3.5g	8.8g
Carbohydrates	16.9g	42.3g
of which sugars	1.8g	4.5g
Fat	0.8g	2.0g
of which saturates	0.2g	0.4g
Fibre	1.5g	3.7g
Sodium	0.2g	0.5g

Word Lists: Thematic

THEME 1
Education, Revise … But Take a Break

advice (n)

advisor (n)

assignment (n)

consider (v)

instructor (n)

intelligence (n)

polite (adj)

relax (v)

respect (v)

brain (n)

forget (v)

memory (n)

remember (v)

revise (v)

term (n)

THEME 2
Daily Life, Parents, Adults and Children. OK?

campus (n)

chess (n)

club (n)

film (n)

music (n)

plan (v)

restaurant (n)

sports (n)

adult (n)

child/ren (n)

husband (n)

parent (n)

relationship (n)

response (n)

wife (n)

THEME 3
Work and Business, How to Make Decisions

applicant (n)

apply (v)

assist (v)

assistant (n)

employ (v)

employee (n)

lead (v)

leader (n)

train (v)

trainee (n)

acronym (n)

decide (v)

evaluate (v)

generate (v)

imagine (v)

process (n)

select (v)

solution (n)

THEME 4
Science and Nature, Chains, Webs and Pyramids

graph (n)

laboratory (n)

science (n)

scientific (adj)

table (n)

test (v)

climate (n)

desert (n)

living thing

plant (n)

polar (adj)

tropical (adj)

THEME 5
The Physical World, Comparing Two Countries

compass (n)

landscape (n)

latitude (n)

location (n)

longitude (n)

region (n)

the Equator (n)

the Middle East

area (n)

border (v)

climate (n)

industry (n)

natural feature

neighbour (n)

population (n)

THEME 6
Culture and Civilization, The Cost of Marriage

celebrate (v)

event (n)

happen (v)

prepare (v)

special (adj)

take place (v)

traditional (adj)

bride (n)

ceremony (n)

groom (n)

husband (n)

marriage (n)

married (adj)

reception (n)

relative (n)

wedding (n)

wife (n)

THEME 7
They Made Our World, Genius and Perspiration

planet (n)

satellite (n)

Solar System

space (n)

star (n)

the Earth (n)

the moon (n)

the sun (n)

device (n)

experiment (v)

invent (v)

invention (n)

inventor (n)

laboratory (n)

materials (n)

patent (n)

telegraph (n)

THEME 8
Art and Literature, *Julius Caesar* and *King Lear*

character (n)

comedy (n)

die (v)

history (n)

literature (n)

play (n)

playwright (n)

tragedy (n)

event (n)

origin (n)

plot (n)

source (n)

theme (n)

THEME 9
Sports and Leisure, When Did They Start?

game *(n)*

land *(v)*

move *(v)*

objective *(n)*

piece *(n)*

play *(v)*

player *(n)*

turn *(n)*

ball game

court *(n)*

kick *(v)*

net *(n)*

pass *(v)*

playing field

post *(n)*

rule *(n)*

team *(n)*

THEME 10
Nutrition and Health, Energy In, Energy Out

biscuit *(n)*

burger *(n)*

cake *(n)*

cereal *(n)*

chip *(n)*

chocolate *(n)*

crisp *(n)*

pasta *(n)*

potato(es) *(n)*

sweet *(n)*

carbohydrate *(n)*

energy *(n)*

fat *(adj)*

fat/s *(n)*

fibre *(n)*

mineral *(n)*

muscles *(n)*

protein *(n)*

vitamin *(n)*

---

acronym *(n)*

adult *(n)*

advice *(n)*

advisor *(n)*

applicant *(n)*

apply *(v)*

area *(n)*

assignment *(n)*

assist *(v)*

assistant *(n)*

ball game

biscuit *(n)*

border *(v)*

brain *(n)*

bride *(n)*

burger *(n)*

cake *(n)*

campus *(n)*

carbohydrate *(n)*

celebrate *(v)*

cereal *(n)*

ceremony *(n)*

character *(n)*

chess *(n)*

children *(n)*

chip *(n)*

---

chocolate *(n)*

climate *(n)*

club *(n)*

column *(n)*

comedy *(n)*

compass *(n)*

consider *(v)*

court *(n)*

crisp *(n)*

decide *(v)*

desert *(n)*

device *(n)*

die *(v)*

employ *(v)*

employee *(n)*

energy *(n)*

evaluate *(v)*

event *(n)*

event *(n)*

experiment *(v)*

fat *(adj)*

fat/s *(n)*

fibre *(n)*

film *(n)*

forget *(v)*

game *(n)*

generate (v)	memory (n)	pole (n)	special (adj)
groom (n)	meridian (n)	polite (adj)	sports (n)
happen (v)	mineral (n)	population (n)	star (n)
history (n)	move (v)	post (n)	stimulus (n)
husband (n)	muscles (n)	potato/es (n)	sweet (n)
imagine (v)	music (n)	prepare (v)	take place (v)
industry (n)	natural feature	process (n)	team (n)
instructor (n)	neighbour (n)	protein (n)	telegraph (n)
intelligence (n)	net (n)	reception (n)	term (n)
invent (v)	objective (n)	region (n)	the Earth (n)
invention (n)	origin (n)	relationship (n)	the Equator (n)
inventor (n)	parent (n)	relative (n)	the Middle East
kick (v)	pass (v)	relax (v)	the moon (n)
laboratory (n)	pasta (n)	remember (v)	the sun (n)
land (v)	patent (n)	respect (v)	theme (n)
landscape (n)	piece (n)	response (n)	traditional (adj)
latitude (n)	plan (v)	restaurant (n)	tragedy (n)
lead (v)	planet (n)	revise (v)	train (v)
leader (n)	plant (n)	rule (n)	trainee (n)
literature (n)	play (n)	satellite (n)	tropical (adj)
living thing	play (v)	select (v)	turn (n)
location (n)	player (n)	Solar System	vitamin (n)
longitude (n)	playing field	solution (n)	wedding (n)
marriage (n)	playwright (n)	source (n)	wife (n)
marry (v)	plot (n)	source (n)	
materials (n)	polar (adj)	space (n)	